Awesome Space

THE SUN AND OTHER STARS

John Farndon

 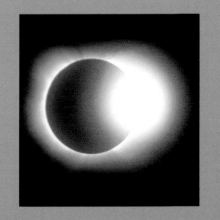 

COPPER BEECH BOOKS
Brookfield, Connecticut

© Aladdin Books Ltd 2001

Produced by:
Aladdin Books Ltd
28 Percy Street
London W1P 0LD

ISBN 0-7613-2412-7

First published in the
United States in 2001 by:
Copper Beech Books,
an imprint of
The Millbrook Press
2 Old New Milford Road
Brookfield, Connecticut 06804

Editor:
Liz White

Designer:
Flick, Book Design & Graphics

Illustrators:
Ian Thompson, Rob Shone,
Graham White, Simon Tegg,
Colin Howard – SGA, Alex
Pang, Richard Rockwood
Cartoons: Jo Moore

Picture research:
Brian Hunter Smart

Certain illustrations have
appeared in earlier
books created by
Aladdin Books.

Cataloging-in-Publication
Data is on file at the
Library of Congress.

Contents

Introduction

Have you ever looked at the awesome stars in the night sky and wondered how they shine? The Sun is our star. It gives us light and heat, but do you know how old it is or how it was born?

This book will propel you into space to explore the Sun and all the stars. Discover what happens during an eclipse, find out why stars seem to twinkle, and learn all about the brightest stars. This book will teach you everything you need to know about the stars, and much more.

Spot and count!

Q: Why watch for these boxes?

A: They give answers to the space questions you always wanted to ask.

zoom in on...

Space bits

Look for these boxes to take a closer look at space features.

Awesome factS

Look for these diamonds to learn more about the truly weird and wonderful facts about the Sun and other stars.

• In this book, a billion is one thousand million.

Stargazing

When you look into the sky on a clear night, you will see thousands of stars. You cannot see them in the daytime since the sky is too bright, but they are still there. The star groups do not change, which makes it easy to learn your way around. You can study the stars with the naked eye, with binoculars, or with a telescope. Never look directly at the Sun.

You do not need any equipment to study the stars. With the naked eye alone you can see the Milky Way, watch for shooting stars, or pick out some of the main star groups.

Looking through binoculars, the Milky Way becomes thousands of individual stars. Some brighter galaxies show up as fuzzy light. You can see more clearly the difference in color and brightness of individual stars.

Looking with a telescope, you can see even more detail. You can see craters on the Moon, and the rings of Saturn. You can also see clouds of dust and gas like the Orion nebula, just below Orion's belt, where stars are being born.

zoom in on...

Candle power

An area of the Sun's surface the size of a postage stamp shines with the power of one and a half million candles! This is why the Sun is bright enough to light up the Earth 93 million miles (150 million km) away.

Every now and then, huge, flamelike looping plumes of hot gas erupt from the Sun's surface (above). These plumes are called solar prominences.

6

Our amazing Sun

The Sun is a star, and like all stars it is a huge fiery ball. The temperature at the center of the Sun reaches over 27 million °F (15m °C)! The Sun is much hotter than any fire on Earth, and is hot enough to melt any known substance. Inside the Sun, one kind of gas is changing into another. This is what makes it shine.

Awesome facts
The Sun weighs 333,420 times more than the Earth and is 110 times wider. In fact, you could fit 1.3 million Earths into the Sun!

Q: What are sunspots?

A: Sunspots are dark patches on the Sun's surface. They look black because they are not as hot as the gas around them. The largest sunspots cover an area 150 times bigger than Earth.

The Sun in the sky

The Sun

The Sun gives off incredible amounts of heat and light in all directions. Only a tiny fraction hits the Earth, but it provides our planet with virtually all its energy. Without the Sun, the Earth would be almost pitch black all the time and colder than the coldest winter imaginable in the Arctic.

Sun's rays

Q: What are the auroras?

A: Auroras are amazing glowing lights that can occur in the skies above the North and South Poles. They are created when streams of electrically charged particles from the Sun enter the Earth's atmosphere.

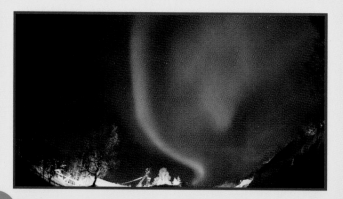

zoom in on...

Equator

The power of the Sun is strongest along the equator, the imaginary line around the middle of the Earth. This is because the equator is the closest point on the Earth to the Sun, so the Sun's rays have less distance to travel.

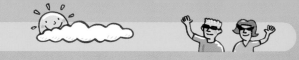

The Earth is surrounded by a magnetic field. This field protects the Earth from the solar wind, a stream of particles that flows from the Sun. When these particles do manage to enter the Earth's atmosphere, usually at the North and South Poles, they cause auroras.

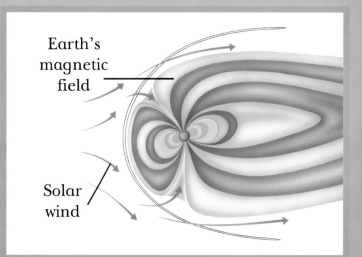

Earth's magnetic field

Solar wind

Day

The Earth spins on its axis while it circles the Sun. This means that while half the Earth faces the Sun and has day, the other half has night.

The equator faces the Sun directly all year.

Night

During a total eclipse of the Sun, the Moon passes exactly in front of the Sun. All that can be seen of the Sun is its corona—its halo of glowing gases. Sometimes, you may see more of the Sun glinting through a valley on the Moon, making it look like a wedding ring with a bright stone.

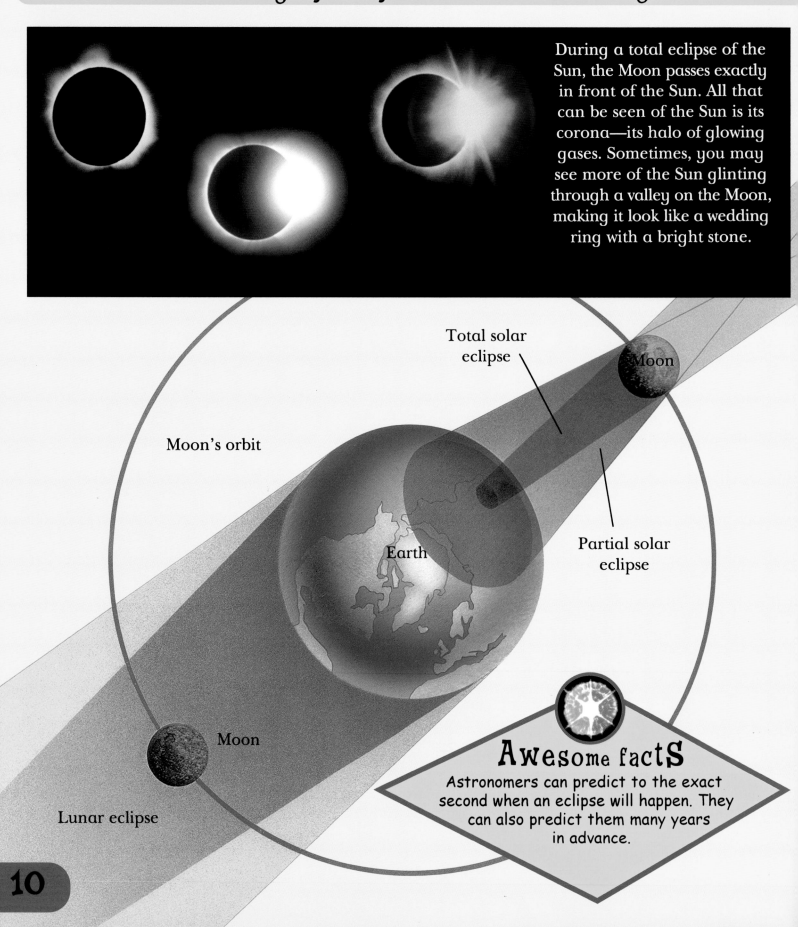

Total solar eclipse

Moon

Moon's orbit

Partial solar eclipse

Earth

Moon

Lunar eclipse

Awesome factS

Astronomers can predict to the exact second when an eclipse will happen. They can also predict them many years in advance.

Sun

Switching the Sun off

Amazingly, because the Sun is so far away, it looks the same size as the Moon in the sky—but it is actually 400 times bigger around! Every now and then, the Moon passes in front of the Sun and blocks it out so that a small area on Earth gets dark during the daytime. This is called a solar eclipse.

zoom in on...

Once or twice in most years, the Moon goes around into the Earth's shadow. This is a lunar eclipse. You see the Earth's shadow as a dark disk creeping across the Moon's face for a few hours. Sometimes the Moon turns deep red.

Chinese dragon swallows the Sun!

Some ancient Chinese believed that during a solar eclipse the Sun was being swallowed by a giant reptile. But Chinese scientists understood and recorded eclipses as astronomical events as long ago as 1360 BC.

Q: How do you find the Pole Star?

A: The Pole Star sits above the North Pole. You can find it by looking for the Big Dipper, a group of seven bright stars shaped like a soup ladle. Then imagine a line joining the last two stars and follow it out to find the Pole Star.

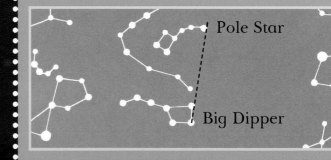

Pole Star

Big Dipper

in on...

Starry tales

Of the 2,000 stars visible with the naked eye, only a few hundred have proper names. Most of the names come from the myths of the ancient Greeks, who believed the night skies told tales, or from the ancient Arabs, who were avid astronomers.

Cygnus the Swan is supposed to be the Greek god Zeus in disguise.

The stargazers of ancient Babylon and Egypt joined stars up into patterns and named them after mythological characters to help remember them. We call these patterns constellations.

Stars in the sky

Look up into the sky on a clear night and you can see lots of twinkling points of light. These twinkling lights are stars like our Sun, only much, much farther away. With a pair of binoculars you can see as many as 5,000 stars! Astronomers guess there are countless trillions out there, too far away to be seen.

Can you spot the Milky Way?

The Milky Way galaxy has 100 billion stars.

Incredible stars

Stars are all huge, fiery balls of gas like our Sun. They shine because they are burning. Stars are so big, pressures deep inside are enough to squeeze atoms so they join together and produce energy in a process called "nuclear fusion"—like a nuclear bomb but billions of times more powerful. The star's center reaches millions of degrees and its surface shines very brightly.

Awesome facts
Inside the biggest stars, temperatures can reach hundreds of millions of degrees, hotter than anything on Earth.

Q: How long have people watched the stars?

A: People have studied the night sky for thousands of years. Some ancient civilizations even thought that the Sun was a god. Early Egyptian astronomers recorded when stars rose and set, and divided the day and night into 12 periods each. They also decorated their temples with constellation gods.

When you look at stars in the sky, their light seems to twinkle and shimmer. Most stars produce an amazingly steady light, but they twinkle because we are seeing them through the thick layers of air above the Earth. When the air moves, the stars seem to shimmer.

Star's light seems to twinkle as it passes through the Earth's atmosphere.

Sirius

Polaris

Venus

How many planets can you see, and how many stars?

Q: How bright are Orion's stars?

A: Orion is easy to spot in the night sky since it has several bright stars. The picture below left shows Orion as it appears in the sky (apparent magnitude). The picture below right, shows how Orion would appear if all the stars were the same distance away (absolute magnitude).

The brightest stars

Some stars seem much brighter than others—sometimes because they are shining brighter, sometimes because they are closer to Earth. A star's "apparent" magnitude is how bright it looks compared to others in the sky. Its "absolute" magnitude tells how bright it really is.

Vega

Spica

Moon

The brighter a star appears, the smaller its apparent magnitude. The brightest thing in the night sky is the Moon, with a magnitude of -12.7. Next comes Venus, which is lit up by the Sun. The brightest star is Sirius. The star Deneb is actually much brighter, but because it is much farther away, it looks dimmer than Sirius.

Moon	-12.7	Vega	0.0
Venus	-4	Spica	1.0
Sirius	-1.5	Polaris	2

Awesome factS

Our Sun is an average-sized star—it will burn for about 10 billion years altogether.

Red star

The color of stars

If you look closely at stars, you can see that their colors vary. For example, Rigel is blue, Sirius is white and Aldebaran is orange. Astronomers have found that a stars's heat, color, and brightness depend upon each other. Hot stars are usually blue or white, and bright. Medium stars are usually yellow and of medium heat and brightness. Cooler stars are usually orange or red, and dimmer.

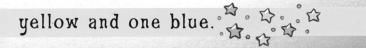
Blue star

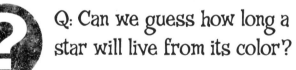

Yellow star

Q: Can we guess how long a star will live from its color?

A: Yes. Blue stars tend to be brighter, but don't live long. Yellow and white stars will burn for about 10 billion years, while red stars are the coolest and will tend to burn longest.

How far to the stars?

Space is much bigger than you can ever possibly imagine, and the stars are huge distances away. The nearest galaxy to ours, the Andromeda galaxy, is so far away that light takes two million years to reach us from there. This means that when astronomers look at it, they are seeing it as it was over two million years ago!

Moon

Sun

1 second

8 minutes

Earth

Q: What is a quasar?

A: Quasar is short for quasi-stellar object. Quasars are incredibly bright objects that astronomers believe to be at the center of very distant galaxies. They are probably the most distant objects astronomers have ever observed.

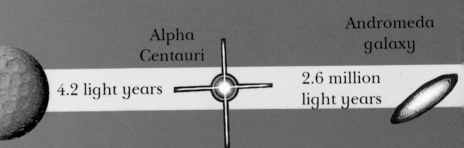

Light year

Because distances in space are so huge, astronomers measure them in light years rather than miles or kilometers. Light is the fastest thing in the Universe, traveling 186,000 miles (300,000 km) in just one second. A light year is the distance light travels in one year, which is nearly 6 trillion miles (9.5 trillion km).

Pluto
5.5 hours

Alpha Centauri
4.2 light years

Andromeda galaxy
2.6 million light years

The illustration shows how long light takes to reach Earth from parts of the Universe. For light, the Moon is just 1.5 seconds away and the Sun is 8 minutes away, but the planet Pluto is 5.5 hours away. The nearest star system, Alpha Centauri, is four years away, and the next galaxy to ours, the Andromeda galaxy, is two million years away!

21

Can you spot the supernovae?

3. Giant star swells to become a supergiant.

4. Medium-sized star collapses to become white dwarf.

2. Giant star starts to swell.

3. Medium-sized star explodes leaving disk of gas and dust.

1. Very bright giant star

2. Medium-sized star swells.

1. Medium-sized star

1. Bright large star

2. Large star starts to swell.

Nebula, the birthplace of stars

22

4. Giant star explodes in supernova.

5. Giant star collapses and creates black hole.

The life of a star

All stars are born in big clouds of dust and gas called nebulae. Stars burn until their fuel is used up. Giant stars swell to an enormous size, explode in a supernova, and collapse to form a black hole. A large star will do the same, but may create a tiny, dense "neutron star" instead of a black hole. Medium-sized stars will swell and explode to leave a white dwarf. Small stars glow dimly for a long time and then cool and fade to a black dwarf.

5. Collapsed large star ends up as a pulsar or neutron star.

4. Large star explodes in supernova.

3. Large star swells to supergiant.

zoom in on...

Supernova!

In 1054 a huge supernova was seen in many parts of the world. A star scratched into stone by Native Americans has been found in present-day New Mexico and is thought to be a record of this supernova event.

Awesome facts
In 1987, the star SN1987A exploded in a supernova. It burned so brightly that it was visible to the naked eye—even though it was in another galaxy.

24

In their last moments, big stars swell until they are supergiants. Pressure in the heart of a supergiant is so huge that gravity squeezes the star and it collapses in an instant to something little bigger than the Earth. At once, it explodes, sending a bright ring of debris and an immensely powerful shockwave rippling out.

Exploding superstars

When a giant star runs out of fuel, it swells up, then collapses in an instant, and blows itself to bits in a gigantic "supernova." Supernovae are rare and brief, but when they occur, they are the biggest firework displays in the Universe. They can burn brighter in a few seconds than our Sun does in 200 million years.

zoom in on...

Pulsar gives off
beams of energy.

Pulsing pulsars

A small, spinning neutron star sometimes lets off flashes of energy as it spins. The energy can be in the form of radio waves or light waves. If Earth lies in the light beam, we see a flashing light that pulses like the light from a lighthouse. This is why these types of stars are called pulsars.

Awesome facts
The Crab Nebula has a pulsar at the center that flashes 30 times a second.

Crab Nebula

Pulsars

When a giant star explodes in a supernova, it sometimes forms a tiny, spinning neutron star. This neutron star is thought to be the tiny core of the star that has been squashed by the explosion. The neutron star spins very rapidly and sometimes gives out a flash of energy. A flashing neutron star is called a pulsar.

Awesome factS

The Crab Nebula is the remains of the supernova that exploded in 1054, and is still giving off 100,000 times as much energy as the Sun.

? Q: What types of nebula are there?

A: Unlike stars, nebulae don't produce light themselves. But reflection nebulae can be seen because the dust in them reflects the light of nearby stars. Glowing nebulae glow red as hydrogen in them is heated by radiation from nearby stars. Planetary nebulae (which have nothing to do with planets) are the flimsy rings of cloud and dust let off when a star dies.

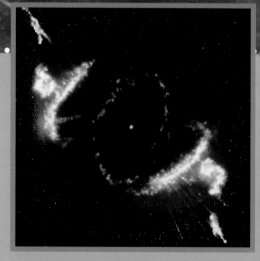

Planetary nebula left behind after a supernova explosion

Can you spot the crab's claws?

Giant clouds

On a clear night, you can see a few fuzzy patches of light. Some of these are distant galaxies, but some are gigantic clouds in space called nebulae. Nebulae are clouds of dust and gas. In some nebulae, gravity squeezes the dust and gas tightly together, and stars are formed.

Reflection nebula reflects light from nearby stars.

Glowing nebula gives out light because gas in it is heated.

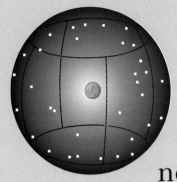

Constellations

People have always made up stories about the stars, linking them into groups and naming them after characters. These groups are called constellations, astronomers recognize 88 in all. You can use these constellations to divide the sky and find your way around from star to star.

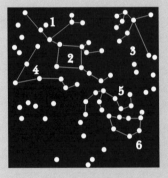

1. Hercules
2. Boötes
3. Ophiucus
4. Aquila
5. Libra
6. Scorpius
7. Sagittarius

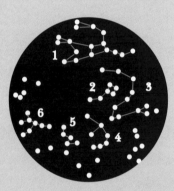

1. Ursa Major
2. Ursa Minor
3. Draco
4. Cepheus
5. Cassiopeia
6. Perseus

1. Andromeda
2. Pegasus
3. Cygnus
4. Aquarius
5. Capricornus
6. Pisces

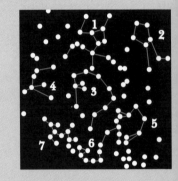

1. Gemini
2. Auriga
3. Aries
4. Taurus
5. Orion
6. Canis Minor
7. Lepus
8. Canis Major

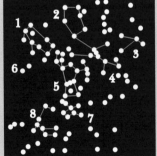

1. Leo
2. Cancer
3. Hydra
4. Corvus
5. Virgo

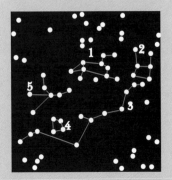

1. Hydrus
2. Pavo
3. Ara
4. Triangulum Australe
5. Octans
6. Musca
7. Crux
8. Volans

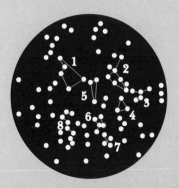

Glossary

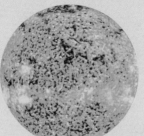

Atmosphere
The layer of gases that surrounds a planet.

Aurora
A bright and colorful glow in the Earth's atmosphere which occurs when particles from the Sun, called the solar wind, enter the atmosphere.

Black hole
The remains of a huge star that has exploded and collapsed in on itself. The gravity is so strong that not even light can escape.

Constellation
A group of stars in the night sky.

Eclipse
When one planet or star passes in front of another. A solar eclipse occurs when the Moon lies between the Earth and the Sun, and a lunar eclipse occurs when the Earth lies between the Sun and the Moon.

Gravity
Every object in the Universe has a force called gravity that attracts it to every other object.

Light year
A unit used to measure distance in space. It is the distance light travels in one year, which is about 6 trillion miles.

Nebula
A cloud of gas and dust, where stars are born.

Neutron star
The remains of a star that has exploded in a supernova.

Nuclear fusion
The process by which atoms are squeezed together until they combine, releasing huge amounts of energy. Fusion occurs inside stars, causing them to shine.

Orbit
The path of one object, such as a planet, around another, like a star.

Pulsar
A neutron star that emits energy as it spins.

Quasar
An object in space that emits an enormous amount of energy. Thought to be at the center of very distant galaxies.

Supernova
When a massive star runs out of fuel it explodes in a supernova explosion.

White dwarf
A small star at the end of its life.

Index

Photocredits
Abbreviations: t-top, m-middle, b-bottom, r-right, l-left, c-center
Cover, 1 all, 2t, 4-5, 6-7, 8tl, 10 all, 11 all, 14-15, 17br, 20ml, 21ml, 21bl, 24-25, 27 tr, 28br, 28-29, 31tr—Corbis. 8bl—Corbis/Royalty Free. 12-13, 18 br—Roger Ressmeyer/CORBIS. 16tl, 24mr—Stockbyte.